GW00706029

NARA

by Shigeru Aoyama

translated
by Don Kenny &
Money L. Hickman

HOIKUSHA

CONTENTS

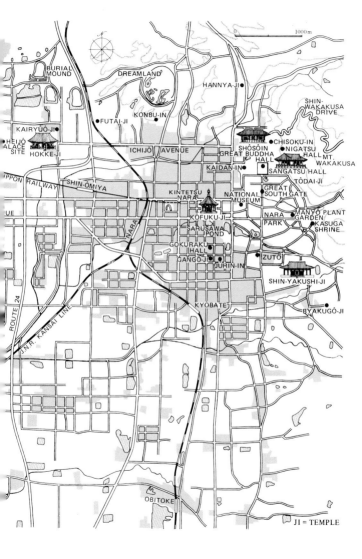

(Cover Photo)
The Five-Storied Pagoda of the Kôfuku Temple and
Sarusawa Pond

N A R A

by Shigeru Aoyama

translated by Don Kenny & Money L. Hickman

© All rights reserved. No. 7 of Hoikusha's Color Books
Series. Published by Hoikusha Publishing Co., Ltd., 17-13,
1-chome, Uemachi, Higashi-ku, Osaka, 540 Japan. ISBN
4-586-54007-9. First Edition in 1964. Eighteenth Edition
in 1984. Printed in JAPAN

The Great South Gate of the Tōdai Temple on a snowy day

The Beautiful Land of Yamato

Yamato is a lovely area. The greatness of its art was produced through a combination of the noble ages of Asuka, Hakuhô, Tempyô, Heian and Kamakura, which extended from the late sixth century to the first half of the fourteenth century. This long history of glory has produced a land of great beauty, which boasts a unique sense of harmony between nature and the handiworks of man.

It was the importation of Buddhist culture from the China mainland during the early days of the history of Yamato that made this land the center of development for the ancient culture of Japan.

Thus for almost a millennium and a half, the land of Yamato has been the "Cradle of Japanese Culture." The center of this lovely land of Yamato is the city of Nara — one of the most beautiful cities in the entire world.

1

The City of Nara

Front View of the Great Buddha Hall of the Tôdai Temple

Emperor Shômu first built the Great Buddha Hall in 745. It was twice destroyed by fire, and the present structure was rebuilted in 1982.

The large octagonal bronze lantern has stood in front of the fifty meter high wooden structure of the Great Buddha Hall ever since it was first constructed.

Octagonal Bronze Lantern

Deva King Gate Guardian (Page 6)

Two ferociously dynamic Deva king statues stand guard on opposite sides of the Great South Gate. These masterpieces of sculpture were carved during the Kamakura Period by Unkei and Kaikei. They are 7.6 meters tall.

Indian Style Brackets of the Great South Gate (Page 7)

This gigantic gate towers over the entrance to the Great Buddha Hall. The Tenjiku (India) style brackets that support the eaves provide an unusual structural beauty. The gate was rebuilt during the Kamakura Period (1192–1333).

Deva King Gate Guardian

Indian Style Brackets of the Great South Gate

Ceremonial Cleaning of the Great Buddha

The Tôdai Temple

Thirty years had passed since the moving of the capital from Asuka to Heijô (present Nara), when an epidemic broke out, in 737, causing heavy loss of life throughout the empire. Emperor Shômu ordered the Tôdai Temple to be built to appease the gods and restore health to the nation. The mobilization of the entire resources of the nation resulted in the creation of a gigantic compound. The fires of war reduced it to ashes, during the last part of the twelfth century and once again during the last part of the sixteenth century. Thus, except for Sangatsu Hall and the Tengai Gate, all the present buildings were reconstructed during the Kamakura (1192–1333) and Edo (1603–1867) Periods, and the total area of the precincts was greatly reduced in size.

The 16 meter high, 500 ton seated bronze statue of the Buddha and the vast wooden hall that houses it are sufficient to give the viewer an idea of the grandeur of the original complex. And together with the statuary found in the Sangatsu Hall and in the Kaidan Monastery, this Daibutsu Statue stands as positive proof of the greatness of the art and craftsmanship of the Tempyô Period (729–764).

Birushana Buddha (Daibutsu)

This immense statue of the Birushana (Vairocana) Buddha is commonly referred to as the Daibutsu. The Buddha is seated with crossed legs and with his hands in gestures that symbolize the control of the entire universe.

The Gigantic Torch showers the Spectators below with Flashing Sparks.

**Annual Torch and
Water-drawing Ceremonies**

The Torch Ceremony (*o-taimatsu*) and the Water-drawing Ceremony (*o-mizu-tori*) are religious rituals that have been carried out annually for nearly a millennium and a half from February 20th through March 14th. The official title of the ceremonies is "The Memorial Service of Nigatsu Hall for the Eleven-Headed Kannon." Beginning on the 20th of February, all priests who are to participate in the cere-

A Strange Tartar Rite carried out inside the Hall

monies take up residence in a special section of the monastery where they are secluded from the secular world under a strictly enforced set of regulations. Here they train and make preparations for the main ritual events which begin on March 1st. On this date, they move to the Nigatsu Hall, where they chant sutras, strike bells, blow conch shell horns, rattle rosary beads, and clank iron staves in ever mounting rhythms, as an accompaniment to the drama of fire and water unfolding outside, without rest until March 14th.

The climax of the ceremonies is reached on the night of March 12th, when gigantic torches are lit and water is drawn from the Wakasa Well beneath the floor of the hall in a secret ceremony, bringing to a close this spectacular festival.

Nigatsu Hall

This hall was built by Priest Jitchû, a disciple of Priest Ryôben, in 752, the same year that the Eye-Opening Ceremony for the Daibutsu was held. The original structure burned to the ground in 1667, and the present building is a faithful reconstruction on the same site. It was built for the purpose of housing a statue of the Eleven-Headed Kannon, and it is known as Nigatsu (February) Hall due to the fact that the ceremonies described on the previous two pages are held there in that month. The front of the building is built as an over-hanging stage, from which an entrancing view of the old capital can be seen.

The name of this hall – Sangatsu (March) – also derives from the fact that an important ritual is carried out within its walls in that month. It is also refered to as Hokke Hall, since it is the Hokke Ceremony that is held there.

Sangatsu Hall is the oldest of all the buildings within the Tôdai Temple precincts. It was built in 729, more than ten years before construction was initiated on the Great Buddha Hall. A small chapel was added during the Kamakura Period, giving the structure its present overall shape.

This Hall houses a veritable galaxy of Tempyô Period (729–764) masterpieces of Buddhist sculpture, including the statue of its main deity the Fukû Kenjaku Kannon (Amoghapasa), along with such other pieces as Bon-ten (Brahma-deva), Taishaku-ten (Sakra Devanam Indra), the Gekkô (Moonlight) Bodhisattva, and the Nikkô (Sunlight) Bodhisattva. A small shrine has been carved in the back of the main statue to house a secret figure of Shitsu-Kongô-Shin (Vajradhara), the doors of which are opened only on December 16th each year.

Sangatsu Hall

The Kôfuku Temple

Among the Seven Great Temples of Nara, the Kôfuku Temple has maintained the closest relationship to the city throughout the centuries, due to its central location. It can even be said that the city of Nara has developed its present shape due to its location and importance, and no account of the medieval history of Japan is complete without a description of the role played by this great temple.

The Five-Storied Pagoda and East Golden Hall (Tô-kon-dô)

The Buildings of the Kōfuku Temple

The Kôfuku Temple was originally built by the wife of Fujiwara Kamatari, and called the Yamashina Temple. In 678, it was moved to Asuka and renamed the Umayasaka Temple. With the establishment of the new capital at Heijô (Nara), in 710, it was moved to its present site and received its present name. As the tutelary temple of the Fujiwara family, its fortunes rose and fell along with those of its patron family. And at the time of the final move of the Imperial capital to Heian (present Kyoto), it enjoyed the greatest prestige of any other temple in the southern area. In spite of numerous burnings and rebuildings, many of its original buildings and sculptures have been preserved.

The building in front of the East Golden Hall is the National Treasure Museum. It is filled with masterpieces of Buddhist art such as the Dry Lacquer Figure of Ashura and the Lantern Bearing Demon.

The Dry Lacquer Figure of Ashura is the most famous of all the statues housed in the National Treasure Museum. It is a product of the Tempyô Period. The space delineated by its six arms, the delicate expressions depicted on its three faces, and its slender standing body never fail to capture the heart of any viewer and leave a strong impression on the mind of even the most discerning of Buddhist sculpture experts.

The Lantern Bearing Demon (Tentô-ki) is Kamakura Period sculpture. Reflecting the social conditions of the age, it has a unique sense of vigor and lucidity. The idea of a hated demon becoming the bearer of a light for the Buddha is typical of the thinking of this period.

Dry Lacquer Figure of Ashura

Lantern Bearing Demon (Tentô-ki)

Bronze Head of Buddha

Statue of Priest Muchaku

The strength and realism expressed in this figure make it one of the greatest masterpieces of Kamakura Period sculpture. It was created by Unkei and his disciples.

The long elegant line of the eyes, the finely shaped nose, and the gentle smile on the lips all contribute to the beauty that makes this head one of the greatest masterpieces of the Hakuhô Period.

19

The Art and Architecture of the Kôfuku Temple

The precincts of the Kôfuku Temple spread over an approximately 436 square meter area. At the height of its prosperity, it boasted some 140 buildings, including worship, lecture, residence, and dining halls, gates, galleries, storehouses, and pagodas. However, it was reduced to ashes numerous times by the fires of war, and the oldest building in the precincts today dates back no further than the Kamakura Period (1192–1333).

On the other hand, the great works of Buddhist sculpture housed here include the Bronze Head of Buddha from the Hakuhô Period, the Tempyô Period dry lacquer figures of Hachibu-shû (the Eight Guardians) and Jû-dai-deshi (the Ten Apostles), and Shi-tennô (the Four Deva Kings) in the East Golden Hall and Jûni-Shinshô (the Twelve Guardians) carved in wood from the Heian Period. Such fine pieces of Kamakura Period sculpture as the Miroku (Maitreya) Bodhisattva in the North Octagonal Hall, portrait statues of Priests Seshin and Muchaku, the Monju (Manjusri) Bodhisattva, the Six Patriarchs of the Hossô Sect, and the pair of Lantern Bearing Demons, Tentô-ki and Ryûtô-ki witness the regaining of power and prosperity experienced by the temple during that period.

The Bronze Head of Buddha was discovered under the pedestal of the principal image during extensive repairs on the East Golden Hall in 1937. It measures approximately one meter in diameter, and the noble features place it in history as a masterpiece of the Hakuhô Period (645–724). Its discovery opened a new page in the history of Japanese sculpture. Records relate that this head is from the principal image of the Yamada Temple in the western part of the Asuka region, and that it was stolen by warrior priests and brought to the Kôfuku Temple during the Heian Period.

Firelight Noh

Firelight Noh

The ritual presentation of Noh performances at the West Golden Hall of the Kôfuku Temple provided the main impetus toward the development and perfection of that art during the Muromachi Period (1394–1466), leading to the formation of the Komparu as well as the other schools of the four Yamato Troupes. Thus it is no exaggeration to state that the ritual Firelight Noh (*takigi-noh*) presentations at the Kôfuku Temple were the very source of this classical style of theatre. Ceremonial performances are still carried out annually in April near the remains of the Great South Gate (Nandai-Mon).

South Octagonal Hall

This hall is situated on a hill beside Sanjô-dôri — one of the city's main thoroughfares. The present building is a 1789 reconstruction.

North Octagonal Hall

This structure was originally built by Empresses Gemmyô and Genshô in memory of Fujiwara Fuhito, in 721. The present building is a reconstruction of the Kamakura Period.

Hanging Lanterns of Kasuga Grand Shrine

Kasuga Grand Shrine

As mentioned earlier, the Kôfuku Temple was the tutelary temple of the Fujiwara family. And Kasuga Grand Shrine enjoyed prosperity in a comparable role as the same family's tutelary shrine. The shrine is recorded to have originated in 768, during the reign of Empress Shôtoku, when the god Takemikatsuchi-no-kami was brought from Kashima on the back of a white deer to take residence at this site. The gods Futsunushi-no-mikoto, Amenokoyane-no-mikoto, and Hime-gami are also enshrined here, and the buildings have been built in such a way that there is a special sanctuary for each deity. These gods are known collectively as the Four Kasuga Myôjin.

The buildings are situated at the foot of Mount Mikasa, surrounded by a virgin forest of cryptomeria, oak and bamboo. The brilliant vermillion of the buildings present an atmosphere of harmony and enchantment as they stand against this background of abundant, rich green.

A famous lantern lighting ritual is carried out here in both

Bugaku Dances performed
▼ at Kasuga Grand Shrine

February and August. The effect created by the lovely glow from the 1,769 stone lanterns and 843 hanging lanterns is one of great mystery and charm. The shrine also boasts a lovely garden, of plants found in the *Manyôshû* Anthology, along the main approach road.

The Row of Stone Lanterns

Wisteria at Kasuga Grand Shrine

◀ The collection of stone lanterns that lines both sides of the Approach Road is the largest in Japan. And they show a high level of design and craftsmanship. There are two basic styles represented here — the Kasuga style and the Oai style. The groupings along both sides of the approach road between the South Gate and the Wakamiya are of particular beauty and charm.

◀ The wisteria blossom is used as the crest of this shrine. And the precincts are famous for the beauty of their, where during the blooming season, the blossoms are so plentiful that one must push the luxurious tassles of blossoms aside to walk through the shrine grounds.

The South Gate

The approach road leads up a gentle incline, between rows of stately stone lanterns.

27

The Inner Gate seen across the Apple Garden

The Main Sanctuary is entirely enclosed within the roofed corridors and the Inner Gate. Thus the Inner Gate itself appears to be the Main Sanctuary. The roofs of the four separate sections of the Main Sanctuary — one for each of the four gods — almost touch each other. They sit in a neat row, with the shrine for Takemikatsuchi-no-kami to the far right of the photograph on page 29.

(above left) The Main Sanctuary
(above right) Arrival of the Imperial Messenger to begin the Saru Festival
(below) The Ceremony under the Pine of the On-matsuri

Festivals of Kasuga Grand Shrine

The three main festivals of Kasuga Grand Shrine are the Saru Festival, the semi-annual Lantern Lighting Ritual, and the popular Wakamiya On-matsuri. The On-matsuri begins with a parade of several hundred people in ancient costumes. The parade ends in front of the Wakamiya Shrine, where such ancient performing arts as Bugaku, Noh, Dengaku, and Sainô are presented.

29

◀ Shiro-Chan

▼ The Deer in Nara Park

The Deer of Nara

"Shiro-Chan" – the Queen of the Deer of Nara

The number of deer in Nara Park comes to around one thousand. The bucks proudly display their antlers, and the does carefully tend their fawns. One doe was born with a crown of white fir on the top of her head. She was extremely popular with tourists, but after only a few short years of life, she was killed in a traffic accident. It seems that a true beauty is fated to a short life even among the deer.

The Antler Cutting Ceremony

Nara's Antler Cutting Ceremony

The deers of Nara Park have enjoyed protection as divine messengers since ancient days. Thus they have become quite tame. However, during the rutting season, the bucks become easily excitable, and during the foaling season, the does become violently protective of their fawns. It is strange to witness the abrupt change in these normally timid and gentle deer.

In order to protect visitors from injury, each fall an Antler Cutting Ceremony is held on Sundays and other holidays. The oldest record of this ceremony is found in an ancient document kept at the Kôfuku Temple, dated 1671. Other documents speak of a great deal of antler cutting during the Genroku Period (1688–1708), but during those days, it was not the organized ceremony it is today.

Three seco are necessary to catch a single buck for the Antler Cutting Ceremony.

Actual Ceremonial Cutting of Antlers

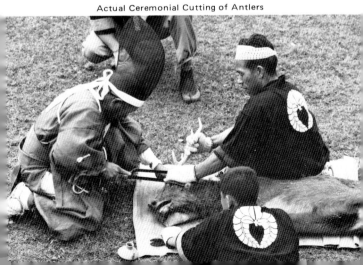

Nara Park

Nowhere else in Japan is nature and history so beautifully preserved as it is in this vast 1,300 acre park, which includes the precincts of the Tôdai Temple, the Kôfuku Temple, and Kasuga Grand Shrine.

Tobihi Plain, situated in the
most inner depths of Nara
Park

Ukimi Hall on Heron Pond ▶

Mount Wakakusa in Spring

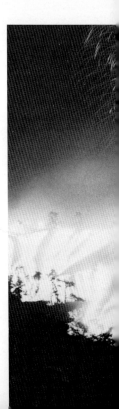

Mount Wakakusa

The greater part of Nara Park is made up of grassy plains and heavily forested mountains. Mount Wakakusa is unique in that it is a gently sloping rise of about 70 acres that is covered with various species of grass. It is 342 meters high at its summit, providing a pleasant afternoon's climb, and a fine view of the entire city of Nara.

At six in the evening on January 15th, conch shell horns are blown, and warrior priests from the Kôfuku Temple set fire to the dry grass on Mount Wakakusa with torches lit at the sacred flame of Kasuga Grand Shrine. They are assisted by several hundred firemen. The fire spreads through the dry grass in an instant, and the mountain is enveloped in a sea of red flame.

Ceremonial Burning of Mount Wakakusa

The Shôsôin Repository is constructed in the Azekura Style of Architecture.

An Earthen Wall surrounds the Shôsôin Repository.

The Shôsôin Repository

On June 21st, 756, the 77th day after the death of Emperor Shômu, Empress Kômyô held a memorial service for him, at which time she dedicated a number of his possessions to the Great Buddha of the Tôdai Temple as a prayer for his happiness in the next world. The Empress dedicated numerous other treasures to the temple on several other occasions, and they were all placed in the Shôsôin Repository for safe keeping. This vast collection has been protected from destruction by both war and natural calamities over the past 1,200 years.

The objects in this fabulous "treasure chest" include writing utensils, musical instruments, costumes, medicines, toys, sutras, weapons, altar fittings, and household furnishings. The total count mounts into the tens of thousands.

The Azekura Style of Architecture

The Shôsôin Repository is a wooden structure, built in a style very similar to that of the American pioneer log cabin. The main difference is that the logs have been cut in a triangular shape. The wood is from a Japanese cypress called *asunaro*. The roof is covered with tiles. This unique construction method was specially devised to maintain a regular level of humidity and temperature inside by means of the natural expansion and contraction of the logs.

Imperial Protection of the Shôsôin Treasures

This building, with its unique construction features and tens of thousands of priceless objects, all perfectly intact after more than 1,200 years, has no parallel anywhere else in the world. Its contents provide us with fascinating examples of the objects in use at court during the 8th century, and demonstrate the overwhelming influence of the superlative culture of T'ang Dynasty China (618–906) on life at the Heijô Capital, where the refined, graceful culture of the Tempyô Period flourished with such splendor and beauty. T'ang civilization had been enriched by many foreign influences, and the Shôsôin collection contains numerous pieces which originated in, or had found their prototypes in Central Asia, Sasanian Persia, India, or the countries of the Eastern Mediterranean Sea. Thus, it is appropriate to regard the Shôsôin Repository as an 8th century Far East terminus of the great Silk Road, which served to link Asia with the Western World from the most ancient times.

Because of the incalculable value of its contents, the Shôsôin Repository has been protected in every possible manner throughout its long existence, and the elaborate rituals and intricate systems used for the sealing and opening of the doors constitutes another one of its fascinating features. An Imperial Messenger's presence is mandatory whenever the seals are applied or removed. The contents were aired annually, beginning in the 9th century, and since the end of the last century, ventilation and inspection have been carried out in accordance with a very regular schedule in November of each year. Two reinforced concrete storehouses have been constructed near the original building, into which the treasures have been moved for greater protection and ease in maintenance.

▲ The Kitayama Leper Sanitorium

Stone Buddha Carv- ▶
ing of the Zutô
Earth Mound

◀ Stone Buddha Head

Stone Buddhas in Nara

Stone Buddha Carving of the Zutô Earth Mound

This bas-relief carving is one of a group of 13 stones from the Nara Period that stand on the three-tiered Zutô Earth Mound — the only one of its kind in Japan. Legend has it that this earth mound was built as the tomb of a Nara Period priest named Genbô (died 746).

The Kitayama Leper Sanitorium and the Stone Buddha Head

Priest Ninshô built this sanitorium during the 13th century to feed, house, and care for those afflicted with leprosy, in the northern part of the city of Nara.

The Stone Buddha Head stands in a grove at the side of the drive that leads past Mount Wakakusa to Kasuga Okuyama. This unusual stone carving is one-meter-high.

The Hannya Temple

The *Taihei-Ki* tells the story of Prince Morinaga, son of Emperor Go-Daigo, who escaped from his pursuers by hiding himself in the sutra box of this temple. But today only the gate (a national treasure of the Kamakura Period) and the dilapidated main sanctuary remain standing, and weeds cover the remainder of the precincts. Still, the stone figures in front of the main sanctuary, and the thirteen-storied stone pagoda with its unique standing stone bodhisattvas remain to tell of its former glory.

Jûrin Monastery

The interior of the main sanctuary of this monastery is built of stone slabs, forming a cavelike atmosphere. The surface of the stone have been carved to form bas-relief figures of the main deity the Jizô (Ksitigarbha) Bodhisattva, flanked by the Miroku (Maitreya) Bodhisattva, Shi-tennô (the Four Deva Kings), and

Standing Stone Bodhisattvas at the base of the Thirteen-Storied Stone Pagoda of the Hannya Temple

several five-storied pagodas. This is the only temple of its kind in Japan.

The Gangô Temple

This is the only one of the Seven Great Temples of Nara that retains all of its original structures. The countless votive stone figures that have been excavated from its precincts seem to be the petrified prayers of the millions of common people who have worshipped here since medieval times.

Wayside Buddhas

Any number of these simple stone figures have stood for centuries in the fields, on the mountains, and along the pathways in and around Nara. They seem to have a depth of compassion and modesty that is somehow lacking in all the grand figures found preserved in the shrines and temples.

The Stone Ksitigarbha Bodhisattva of Jûrin Monastery

Main Sanctuary ▶
of Jûrin
Monastery

The tiles with thick outer ends and the special way of laying them are unique to this temple.

Originally a residence hall for monks, the Paradise Chamber was later rebuilt as two buildings — one the main sanctuary and the other the Zen meditation hall. This temple has been a center of worship for the common people since medieval times.

▲ Roof Tiles (above) and the Paradise Chamber of ▶
the Gangô Temple (below right)

The Takahata Area

The ancient capital city of Nara, with its traditional atmosphere of peace and serenity, has changed in recent years. The center of the city is filled with noise and exhaust fumes. But one can escape these conditions by going a short distance into the suburbs, to such regions as Takahata, where a mood of unspoiled tranquility prevails. If one ventures a bit further along the road from Takahata to the Byakugô Temple at the foot of Mount Takamado, one finds that the fresh fragrance of centuries past is still strong.

A Rustic Earthen Wall in the Takahata Area

The Main Sanctuary of the Shin Yakushi Temple

The Shin Yakushi Temple

Just outside the inhabited part of the Takahata Area stands the silent Shin Yakushi Temple. It was built by Empress Kômyô as a plea to the gods for the restoration of the health of Emperor Shômu. The Main Sanctuary has stood as it exists today since it was first built in the Nara Period. The main image of the Yakushi (Bhechadjaguru) Nyorai (Tathagata) sits on a circular white mortar dais in the center of the Main Sanctuary surrounded by a complete set of life-sized statues of Jûni-Shinshô (the Twelve Guardians). One of this group is a wood carving and was a later addition, but the other eleven are fine examples of Tempyô Period art.

There is talk recently of selling one or two of the minor Kannon images owned by the temple in order to help make ends meet. What a sad fate for such a lovely temple!

The Main Sanctuary of the Futai Temple and the Forsythia
Blossoms

Saho Road

Ichijô Avenue, which runs directly east from the archaeological site of the Heijô Palace grounds, is also known as Saho
Road. It connects the Tôdai Temple with a Buddhist nunnery of
the same period known as the Hokke Temple.

Also situated along this road are the Konpu Monastery, the
Futai Temple, and the Kairyûô Temple. The Konpu Monastery,
originally erected in 771 by order of Fujiwara Momokawa, a
state minister, is a nunnery, and contains a fine garden laid out
by the famous garden master Kobori Enshû during the early
17th century.

West Golden Hall of the Kairyûô Temple and Blossoming
Willows

Flowers bloom in Profusion in All Four Seasons at the Futai Temple.

The Futai Temple was used as a residence by Emperor Heijô (reigned 806–809) after he abdicated, and the famous 9th century poet and romantic figure Ariwara-no-Narihira is also said to have lived there, for which reason it is also known as the Ariwara Temple.

Located at the northeast end of the ancient palace grounds, the Kairyûô Temple was originally constructed under Empress Kômyô's orders, and was made the headquarters for nunneries throughout the nation. It continues to function as a nunnery even today, and one immediately senses an atmosphere of refinement and grace upon entering the compound.

Proceeding farther west along Saho Road, one passes the Saidai Temple and the Akishino Temple. While enjoying the charms of these ancient temples, one must also take care not to miss the grand burial mounds found along this same road. Together they are known as the Saki Burial Mound Group. In this group are the Uwanabe Mound, the Konabe Mound, the Princess Iwa Mound, the Emperor Heijô Mound, the Princess Hihasu Mound, and the Emperor Seimu Mound. Along with the larger key-hole shaped mounds of the 4th century, these are a part of the larger ancient burial mound area that is attracting a great deal of interest in the field of archaeology in recent years.

The Precincts of the Hokke Temple have an Elegance Appropriate to a Nunnery.

The Garden of the Hokke Temple

The Hokke Temple

This temple enjoyed great prosperity during the Nara Period, but now all that remains is the Main Sanctuary which was built in the Kamakura Period, the South Gate and the Bell Tower which were built in the Momoyama Period, and the Guest House and the Monks' Living Quarters which were moved to this site from the Kyoto Imperial Palace during the middle of the Edo Period. The garden is made of stones, with a path connecting all parts for the enjoyment of the viewer. One of the garden's particularly lovely features is the irises that grow beside the fountain in the center.

The Eleven-Headed Kannon — the Main Deity
of the Hokke Temple

Legend has it that the Eleven-Headed Kannon was carved
by an Indian artist who used Empress Kômyô as his model.
However, sculpture historians believe that it is an early Heian
Period piece carved by a master sculptor from a single piece
of Japanese cypress (*hinoki*) wood.

The Heijô Palace Grounds

1,250 years ago, the Imperial Palace and court compound were located in the area shown in the center of this photograph. In the Spring of 710, while the various extensive public works and construction projects necessary for a new capital were still in progress, Empress-Regent Gemmyô transferred her court from the Asuka Area to this new site. It remained the seat of the government until 784, when Emperor Kanmu moved the capital to Kyoto. Between these years, seven sovereigns reigned, and the richly varied culture of the Tempyô Period came into full flower and flourished on a scale unprecedented in Japan. At the same time, various factions among the nobility competed for authority, and intrigues were the standard occurrences of the day. Although the political developments of the period were marked by conspiracy and frequent bloodshed, the cultural achievements of the era are among the most remarkable in the long span of Japanese history.

The Stone Marker at the Heijô Palace Grounds

Laid out in imitation of the great Chinese capital, Ch'ang-an, the metropolis stretched 4.2 kilometers east to west, and 4.7 kilometers north to south. Coherence and symmetry, still apparent in the layout of the city of Nara, were foremost in the minds of the planners. The city was divided vertically into two main blocks by a broad central thoroughfare, and main avenues were established on a regularized grid-plan, with the result that the capital resembled an oblong chess-board.

In the shadow of the seemingly great prosperity demonstrated by the bustling activity of this grand scale construction project, there were many common people who died or ran away due to the gruelling forced labor imposed upon them, and there were serious epidemics and destruction of crops throughout the country. But the glory of Tempyô Culture was sufficient to overshadow all these disasters.

Site of the Ancient Chôdô Monastery

The Chôdô Monastery was the site of rituals and important affairs of state. It stood close to the Great Hall of State and the Audience Hall.

Today, almost the entire site of the palace grounds has been obtained by the government and plans are in progress to make it a national historical park.

Site of the Audience Hall

Excavated Site of an Ancient Well

Vast Rows of Post Holes

Excavation of the Heijô Palace Grounds

In 1959 a comprehensive plan for the excavation of this site, to reveal the secrets of this city which had slept beneath the ground for centuries, was initiated by the government, for the purpose of collecting academic data. The ditches and post holes of a vast palace structure were revealed, along with countless utensils, *Wadô-kaihô* coins, and wooden tablets covered with various messages. Thus the site has become the underground treasure house of ancient Japan, comparable in historical, archaeological, and cultural value to the Shôsôin Repository.

Uwanabe Mound and Konabe Mound (left rear)

Saki Burial Mound Group

The fact that the Saki Burial Mound Group near the northern end of the Heijô Palace Grounds is very important to the field of archaeology has been mentioned earlier. In the *Shoku Nihongi*, it is mentioned that some of the more ancient mounds were destroyed to build the Heijô Capital, and this has been verified by the excavations that have been carried out there in recent year. The Emperor Heijô Mound is at present circular in shape, but it has been discovered that it was originally a 200 meter long keyhole-shaped mound and that its narrow long tail section was taken away to make room for the construction of the palace grounds.

Gigantic utensils
are used in the Tea
Ceremony Festival
at the Saidai Temple

Remains of the
▼ East Pagoda

Image of the Angel named Gigei-ten at the Akishino Temple

Magnolias blooming at the
▼ Akishino Temple

Nishi-no-Kyô Area

The Saidai Temple

During the middle of the Nara Period, at the time when Fujiwara-no-Nakamaro and Priest Dôkyô were struggling against each other for supreme power, Empress Shôtoku established this temple in 765 in order to counterbalance the overwhelming power of the great Tôdai Temple. The great scale and number of buildings in the original complex indicate that it was equal to its intended task. The name Saidai (Great Western) Temple was meant to indicate its purpose in relation to the Tôdai (Great Eastern) Temple. Its fortunes declined in the centuries to follow, and it was ravaged by a series of disastrous fires, to the point that today a desolate atmosphere pervades its precincts. However, its museum and Main Sanctuary contain a great number of valuable works of art, including paintings, sculpture, and objects of craftwork.

During the middle of April every year, an amusing festival is held here, known as the Great Tea Ceremony (*Ô-cha-mori*). Tea is made in a tea cup that is a full meter in circumference, with a tea whisk that is as big as a broom. The festival is said to have originated in the Kamakura Period in connection with the Kôshô Bodhisattva. Legend has it that when the Kantô Area army was on its way home from the war with Mongolia in 1274, they stopped by this temple to participate in this festival, and that while they had not been surprised by the great army of the Mongolians, they were shocked speechless by the size of the tea cup.

The Main Sanctuary and the Stone Lantern of the Akishino Temple

The Akishino Temple

Emperor Kônin, the last ruler of the Nara Period, established this temple in 780, just four years before the capital was
moved to Kyoto, making it literally the last temple built during
the Nara Period. The present Main Sanctuary dates from the
Kamakura Period, but it follows the Nara Period prototype
very closely.

The majority of visitors come to see the famous image of
the angel named Gigei-ten. The head was made of dry lacquer
during the Nara Period, and the body is a wood carving of the
Kamakura Period. The joining of the two disparate parts has
been accomplished in such a way that a great work of art
has thus been created. The gently inclined head gazes
benevolently downward, giving the whole figure an elegant
sensuality. The temple's collection also includes such Important
Cultural Assets as figures of Daigensui Myô-ô (the Great
Warrior God), Bon-ten (Brahma-deva), Taishaku-ten (Sakra
Devanam Indra), the Eleven-Headed Kannon, and the Gudatsu
Bodhisattva.

The Golden Hall through the Great South Gate

The Golden Hall of the Tôshôdai Temple is the only one of its kind that remains in its original state since the Nara Period. The Triple Hand Breadth Brackets and the entasis of the support posts give the structure the dignity and serenity of Tempyô Period architecture. And the Ornamental Ridge-end Tiles placed at both ends of the peak of the roof add strength to the overall design of the building.

The Ornamental Ridge-end Tile of the Golden Hall

Road to the East Gate of the Tôshôdai Temple

Precincts of the Tôshôdai Temple: (From left to right) the Golden Hall, the Lecture Hall, and the Drum Pavilion

The Tôshôdai Temple

The renowned Chinese priest Chien-chen (Ganjin) came to Japan to supervise the ordination and training of monks upon the invitation of Emperor Shômu. He was determined to travel to Japan despite the reluctance of his followers and the opposition of Chinese officials, and he first embarked on his journey in 742. However, he did not set foot on Japanese soil until 753. In the meantime, he had made five unsuccessful attempts at the crossing, all of which failed due to skirmishes with pirates, shipwreck, and storms. On top of all this hardship, his eyesight failed, and he was totally blind by the time he finally reached the Heijô Capital.

On his sixth attempt, he was successful in landing on Okinawa and making his was across Kyûshû to his destination. Eleven years had passed since he had made his decision to visit Japan, and he had reached the age of 67 by the time of his ultimate arrival. Emperor Shômu and Empress Kômyô greeted him warmly and lodged him at the recently dedicated Tôdai Temple. A seat of ordination was set up for him in the Great Buddha Hall, and Chien-chen performed the rites that marked the first introduction of the Ritsu Sect of Buddhism into Japan.

However, the scholarly monk soon found the intrigue and power struggles which centered around the Tôdai Temple an uncongenial atmosphere in which to practice the tenets of his faith. Thus he was granted possession of the old mansion of Prince Nitabe at the western edge of the city, at which site he built the Tôshôdai Temple, where he went to spend the remainder of his life.

Inside the Golden Hall stands the 3.3 meter high dry lacquer figure of the temple's main deity the Birushana (Vairocana) Buddha, flanked by a 5.4 meter high figure of the

Mid-Autumn New Moon

meter high figure of the Yakushi (Bhechadjaguru) Nyorai (Tathagata) to the right. Amongst this group are more than 2 meter high figures of Bon-ten (the Brahma-deva), Taishaku-ten (the Sakra Devanam Indra), and Shi-Tennô (the Four Deva Kings). All of these statues have been preserved since they were originally created for this temple. Their conglo-merate mass is overwhelming. They seem to fill the huge Golden Hall to overflow-ing. The temple also owns several wooden statues of note, which are kept in its new museum.

An Arm of the Thousand-Armed Kannon

The Standing Headless
Wooden Nyorai Figure

The Birushana Buddha, flanked by the Thousand-Armed Kannon on the left and the Yakushi Nyorai on the right

The Buddhist figures of the Tôshôdai Temple mentioned on page 69 were carved by Chien-chen's disciples who came from China with him. For this reason, they have a marked difference in atmosphere from those statues found in the Sangatsu Hall of the Tôdai Temple and in the various buildings of the Kôfuku Temple. Thus they give the Tôshôdai Temple a distinct flavor of its own.

The standing headless wooden Nyorai (Tathagata) figure seen on page 70 is no less than the 'Venus of the Orient.' Perhaps the loss of its head has added to the effect of its great beauty. This is the finest example of the Tôshôdai Temple style of wood carving.

The Yakushi Temple

A ten minute stroll from the South Gate of the Tôshôdai Temple brings one to the Yakushi Temple. This temple was established by Emperor Tenmu south of Mount Miminashi near the Imperial Palace to pray for a cure for his Empress, soon after he had defeated his older brother Emperor Tenchi in 672. However, before construction was completed, Emperor Tenmu himself died, and his Empress who had recovered her health succeeded him to the throne, taking the name Jitô. Empress Jitô had the temple completed, after she took the

Finial on Top of the East Pagoda

The Precincts of the Yakushi Temple seen from Katsumata Pond

throne, in memory of her husband. Thus it was finally completed 17 years after work on it had begun.

In 710, when the capital was moved from Asuka to Heijô, the Yakushi Temple was moved to its present site. The three-storied East Pagoda is the only original building still remaining in the precincts today. It is topped by a delicate cast-bronze finial of great beauty, showing twelve Buddhist celestials playing musical instruments, which has been deservedly praised as 'frozen music.'

There is also a collection of Buddhist sculpture that is the pride of ancient Japanese art historians, which includes the main bronze triad of the Yakushi Nyorai, flanked by the Gakkô Bodhisattva and the Nikkô Bodhisattva, as well as the magnificent standing Shô-Kannon figure and the painting of Kichijô-ten (the Sri-maha-devi).

This is actually a three-storied pagoda, but due to the special construction method of placing an extra set of eaves between each story, it appears to have six stories.

East Pagoda of the Yakushi Temple

The Golden Hall of the Yakushi Temple

The Golden Hall of the Yakushi Temple was restored to its original appearance in April of 1976. The reconstruction work costs two billion yen. Its style of construction is similar to that of the East Pagoda in that it has an extra set of eaves between each level, making it appear to have four levels.

75

The Main Image of Yakushi Nyorai

As Fenollosa gazed into the face of this statue, he exclaimed, "The time and money I spent coming to Japan has been repaid by the opportunity it afforded me to see this figure." And Okakura Tenshin is quoted as having said, "I envy anyone who has yet to experience the great joy of seeing that statue for the first time."

The Tôin Hall where the Shô-Kannon Figure is housed

The bronze has taken on a deep black sheen, as though it has been carefully pollished. This perfectly formed 3 meter high figure is a masterpiece of ancient Japanese art, but its creator's name is unknown.

The Left Hand of the Main Image

Foreign Figures on the Pedestal of the Main Image

This pedestal is famous for its exquisite design and its cultural value. The half-naked dwarflike men seem to be from the South Seas. They symbolize the cultural integration of East and West.

◀ Painting of Kichijô-ten

This portrait of Kichijô-ten (the Sri-maha-devi) was done with oil-base paints on linen. It is one of the very few existing examples of Nara Period painting. It is only 53 centimeters in height and 32 centimeters in width, but because of its great artistic dignity, it gives the impression of being much larger.

The Gakkô Bodhisattva and Other Treasures of the Yakushi Temple

A large crack appeared in the neck of this 3 meter high figure during the severe earthquake at Yoshino in 1952. Specialists of the Cultural Properties Commission severed the inner supports and removed the head. When this came to the attention of the general public, it caused quite a furor, and the matter of whether or not repairs should be made was finally taken up in the National Diet.

It was finally decided to utilize aircraft construction technology to insert a stainless steel frame to replace the head. Further repairs were carried out on the main pedestal. The entire project required a full 6 years for completion.

Repairing of the Head of the Gakkô Bodhisattva

The Yakushi Temple also houses a number of other valuable works of art and objects of historical importance. The Shô-Kannon image in the Tôin Hall is a bronze figure that was cast 30 years earlier than, in the Hakuhô Period. However, there is a theory that it was made in the Tempyô Period. In any case, it is a piece of great importance to the history of Japanese art. There are also three small wooden Shintô portrait figures from the early Heian Period of an Emperor, a royal princess and the god Hachiman. These are important due to the scarcity of example of Shintô art.

Two Annual Ceremonial Events

Emperor Horikawa's (reigned 1029-1107) consort took ill. She recovered as a result of the Emperor's fervent prayers. A Buddhist service was held in gratitude in which women of the imperial court made ten different kinds of artificial flowers, including plum, peach and cherry to offer to the Yakushi Nyorai. This service has been held annually since that time from the 30th of March to the 5th of April, and is known as the *Hana-e-shiki*. Another event is carried out at the end of every year and once again before the above ceremony, in which the bronze surface of the Yakushi Nyorai image is cleaned. It is called the *O-mi-nugui*.

Ceremonial Cleaning of the ▲ Yakushi Nyorai Figure

The Yakushi Nyorai Figure decorated with artificial Flowers ▼

Ikaruga Village

It is said that speckled pidgeons used to inhabit this area. Prince Shôtoku built his Ikaruga (literally 'speckled pidgeon') Mansion here and commuted to the ancient Asuka Capital.

The Hôryû Temple

   Ikaruga Village contains the oldest extant temple buildings
in all Japan. And the works of painting, sculpture and craftsmanship which are preserved there cover the entire history of
Japanese art, from the Asuka through the Edo Periods, making
it both a Mecca for Japanese cultural history scholars and a
bustling tourist center for visitors from both at home and
abroad.

The Road from the Sai-in to the Tô-in

According to tradition, Emperor Yômei (father of Prince Shôtoku) fell ill in 587. Prince Shôtoku and the Emperor's younger sister (who later became Empress Suiko) prayed fervently for his recovery. The monarch died, but in 607, Prince Shôtoku completed this temple and dedicated it to his memory. The date is inscribed on the nimbus of the main image in the Golden Hall.

However, the *Nihon Shoki* states that all the buildings were burned to the ground when the precincts were struck by lightening in 670. This record has caused a great deal of controversy among modern scholars. One group contends that the record is unreliable and that the building extant today as those that were built in 607, and the opposing group maintains that the present buildings are reconstructions of the originals, which were built after the conflagration of 670.

Beyond controversy, however, is the fact that the Middle Gate, the Corridors, the Golden Hall, and the Five-Storied Pagoda clearly represent the architectural style of the Asuka Period, and that they may well be the oldest wooden buildings in the entire world.

The temple precincts are divided into two compounds — the main area called the Sai-in (West Monastery), and the Tô-in (East Monastery) that was built by Priest Gyôshin in 739, on the site of Prince Shôtoku's Ikaruga Mansion, in memory of that great prince, centered around the Hall of Dreams. Recent excavation has revealed that there was also a compound known as the Wakakusa Precincts, located between the Sai-in and the Tô-in, and older than either of them.

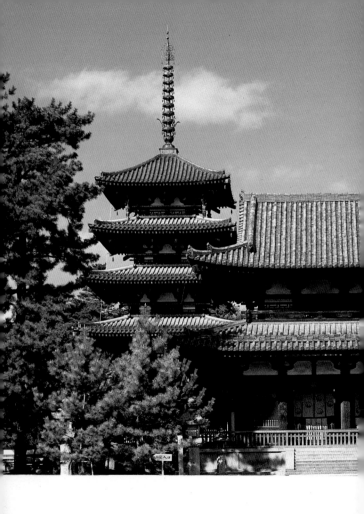

The precincts of the Sai-in are filled with buildings that are of the multiple-tiered Asuka style of architecture – the Middle Gate, the Golden Hall, the Pagoda and the Corridors.

The Golden Hall, which is built upon a double foundation, is constructed in a multi-level style with eaves. The entasis of the pillars, the 'cloud' brackets, and the stylized swastika pattern of the railings are all examples of the Asuka style of architecture. These are the oldest buildings in all of Japan.

The Golden Hall in ▶
the Center of the
Hôryû Temple

Mural Painting of the Golden Hall (before the 1949 fire)

Bronze Figure of the Yume-chigae Kannon

The Sculpture of the Golden Hall

To the right of the Shakyamuni Triad is a seated figure of the Yakushi Nyorai. There is also Nara Period group of Shi-tennô (the Four Deva Kings). Also there are the twelve mural paintings on the walls that have finally been restored to their original state after having been heavily damaged by a tragic fire some years ago. And in the treasure storeroom, there are also such famous works of art as the Kudara Kannon, the Yume-chigae Kannon, the Tamamushi Miniature Shrine, and the Nine-Headed Kannon.

The Shakyamuni Triad

An inscription on the back of the nimbus of this Triad
states that it was created by Buddhist sculptor Tori in answer
to a commission from certain aristocrats, one year after the
death of Prince Shôtoku, and that is was dedicated to that
prince's memory.

The Hall of Dreams (Yume-dono)

Visitors never tire of comparing the real thing with its picture on Japan's ten thousand yen bill. The fact that it was chosen to be depicted in this manner attests to its great universal beauty and the value placed on it by the nation of Japan.

The American scholar Ernest Fenollosa was the first to reveal this ancient 'secret image' (*hibutsu*) to the modern world when he carefully unwrapped the some 90 meters of white cloth in which it had been encased for centuries. Thus the fresh brilliance of its gold plating cuts across the 1,300 years since it was created to give the viewer direct contact with the ancient past. The general public is given a chance to view the dazzling beauty of this statue in the Spring and the Autumn of every year.

The Kuze Kannon

The Temples of Ikaruga Village

Although the Hôryû Temple is traditionally the most closely associated with the name of Prince Shôtoku and his family, a number of other temples in the Ikaruga neighborhood are also identified with this great nobleman.

The Chûgû Temple, a nunnery, lies hidden behind and just to the east of the Tô-in compound which centers around the Hall of Dream. According to tradition, the residence of Prince Shôtoku's mother was converted into a nunnery in order to pray for her salvation and subsequently given the name Chûgû Temple. Its original site seems to have been located some 300 meters to the east, and the transfer to its current location appears to have been carried out much later. The traditions of this temple have been carefully handed down over the centuries. Thus even today, it has an atmosphere of fastidious order and refinement that is striking.

The main image is thought to be of the Nyoirin Kannon, but there are some who believe it to represent the Miroku (Maitreya) Bodhisattva. In any case, it has always been of great interest to Japanese art historians and a source of inspiration to pilgrims who journey to the temple.

The Chûgû Temple also possesses the oldest piece of embroidery in Japan — a scene from the Celestial Longevity Mandala (*Tenju-koku Mandara*), which was created by Lady Tachibana, the wife of Prince Shôtoku, after his death.

One kilometer northeast of the Chûgû Temple, situated in the midst of a secluded grove of pines, stands the Hôrin Temple, which was founded in 622 by Prince Shôtoku's eldest son. Its Nara Period Three-storied Pagoda was destroyed by lightening in July of 1944, but it has now been reconstructed. The Treasure Storehouse built on the remains of the old Lecture Hall contains many notable works of art including

The Three-Storied Pagoda of the Hôki Temple

two examples from the Asuka Period — the standing Kannon and the Yakushi Nyorai which is the temple's main image — as well as the Miroku (Maitreya) Bodhisattva and the Eleven-Headed Kannon from the early Heian Period.

A few hundred yards east of the Hôrin Temple, close to the palace where Prince Shôtoku expounded on the profundities of the Lotus Sutra, stands the Hôki Temple. This temple's Asuka Period Pagoda is the oldest and tallest (24 meters) three-storied specimen in Japan, and is regarded as the finest example of its kind. In addition to temples, a number of other historical sites are located in the Ikaruga neighborhood, such as the kiln locations where roof tiles of the local temple buildings were fired beginning in the Asuka Period, and the burial mound of Prince Shôtoku's eldest son.

The Nyoirin Kannon — Main Image of the Chūgū Temple

The prayers offered during the 1,300 years since the Asuka Period have polished the surface of this figure, producing a deep black lustre.

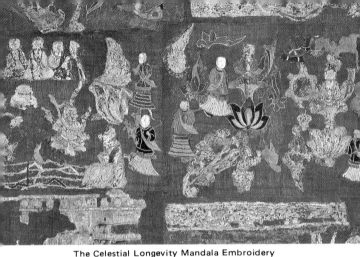

The Celestial Longevity Mandala Embroidery

▲ This one meter square piece of embroidered tapestry is only a fragment of the original, but it is sufficient to remind the viewer today of the splendor it must have had.

Two generations of head ▶ priests worked diligently to collect funds for the re-building of this pagoda that had been destroyed by fire. Their dreams were finally realized in 1975,

The Three-storied Pagoda of the Hōrin Temple

The Monument for Dr. Langdon Warner

Dr. Langdon Warner

The cities of Nara and Kyoto, with their ancient temples and treasures, were spared from destruction during the Pacific War, thanks to the determined efforts of the noted American scholar of Far Eastern Art, Dr. Langdon Warner. He is credited with having drawn up a list of areas in which cultural assets were located, and in intervening with high government and military officials to prevent their destruction by bombing. The extent of his grief must have been profound when he heard the news of the tragic fire in 1949 which seriously damaged the great murals at the Golden Hall of the Hôryû Temple — a temple of which he was particularly fond. He spent some years pursuing his research in Japan, and is well known for his penetrating, yet sympathetic studies on Far Eastern Art. When he passed away in 1955, a monument was erected in his memory at a secluded, pine-shaded location in the northwest corner of the compound. From its slight elevation, a fine view of the five-storied pagoda that he loved so well can be seen.

NARA AND THE MANYÔSHÛ ANTHOLOGY

The oldest and most voluminous of extant anthologies of Japanese poetry is the *Manyôshû* (Collection of Ten Thousand Leaves), a compilation in twenty books, comprising about 4,500 poems, which appears to have been assembled in its present form about the year 759. It includes a few poems which may have been composed as early as the fourth century, but it is clear that the majority were written during the period of about 100 years preceding the compilation, at a time when influences from the Asiatic mainland, then dominated by the superlative civilization which flourished under the T'ang Dynasty (618-906), were particularly strong in Japan. The Chinese system of writing had arrived earlier, probably indirectly through Korea, and seems to have been in very limited use as early as the fifth century. With the introduction of Buddhism into Japan in the succeeding century, however, the study of Chinese became essential, and as growing numbers of native scholars struggled to unravel its complexities, interest in the institutions, philosophies, literature and arts of China also grew with an ever-increasing momentum. There can be little doubt that the example of Chinese literature served as a stimulus to the growth of Japanese poetry, and that it influenced the production of the elegant and varied works collected in the *Manyôshû* in a number of ways. At the same time, however, the sentiments expressed in the *Manyôshû* are essentially Japanese, so much so that the anthology might be called almost purely Japanese in content without risk of criticism. There is a fine admixture of the powerfully direct and spontaneous with the rich and elegant in the imagery and rhythms of these poems which disappears in large part in the literary works of subsequent periods when forms became regularized, and the standards of emotion in poetic expression tended to become debilitated and over-refined.

The authors of the *Manyôshû* poems were, for the most part, members of what clearly was an educated and aristocratic elite. A number of their names are known, and their positions as nobles closely associated with the Japanese court can be presumed with confidence. It is true that there are a few examples, mainly in a group known as the *Azuma-uta* (Songs of the East), which are products of anonymous poets and have a rustic, simple, unaristocratic flavor about them which seems unassociated with the sentiments of the nobility, but these are only a small part of the total.

Archaeological evidence shows that the main center of the mixed bronze and iron culture of the proto-historic period in Japan had become centered in the region of the Yamato Plain by the third century A.D. In this sheltered basin, east of present Osaka, which is frequently referred to as the "Cradle of Japanese Civilization," a distinctive culture and society gradually developed, dominated by a central authority which emerges with the first reliable historical records as the Imperial Clan. The number and considerable size of the burial mounds of the sovereigns and members of the aristocracy which dot the region is impressive evidence of their power, and the relics excavated from their tomb chambers — superbly executed weapons, armour, jewelry, horse trappings, and other rich accessories — demonstrate the artistic and technical progress which took place over several centuries. At this time, probably because of ritual taboos associated with pollution, custom seems to have required that the residence of a sovereign be abandoned after his death, and a new structure erected for the successor at a different location. As a result of the gradual introduction of Chinese ideas after the middle of the sixth century, however, the concept of a permanent capital centering on the monarch's palace seems to have eventually reached Japan. The first efforts to achieve this ideal may be seen at a site in the Asuka district in the southern part of the Yamato Plain, where the capital known as Fujiwara was laid out in imitation of a continental model during the reign of the Empress Jitô (r. 686-697). The site was abandoned shortly afterward, however, and the transfer of the capital to Heijô ("Citadel of Peace", present Nara) in 710 marks the first completion of a permanent capital based on Chinese ideas of city planning to be carried out in Japan. Heijô was to remain the capital until 784, and during these years, the Japanese made such remarkable progress in learning and the arts that the Tempyô Period stands as one of the greatest epochs in Japanese civilization. Court life became established on a firmer and more elaborate basis during Tempyô times, and with these developments came greater urbanity and refinement. One of the requisites of the courtiers of the day was the ability to compose verse, and many of the lovely scenic locations around Nara are described with impressive imagery and power in the *Manyôshû* poems.

During the eighth century, one of the main thoroughfares running east and west across Heijô Capital was Sanjô-ôji. Today, as one passes out of the main Kintetsu-Nara Station and up the incline past the rows of souvenir stalls and hotels to the Kôfuku Temple compound, he proceeds along the same historic street. If one continues, he soon arrives at a red *torii*-gate which marks the beginning of the approachway to Kasuga Shrine, which lies hidden in a thick stand of dark trees further up the hill. On both sides lie wide grassy meadows, accented by the shadows of occasional cypresses and maples. During the Tempyô Period the fields in this area Kasuga Plain, Asaji Plain, and Tobihi Plain were favorite recreation spots for the courtiers, and they are mentioned in a number of the *Manyôshû* poems. Today, however, the clientele has changed, and on a warm Sunday these same fields are filled with families, company groups, and couples who have brought picnic-lunches, and are enjoying a day of relaxation in Nara. Always a part of this scene are the Nara deer, close by, waiting for a chance to participate in one of the more sumptuous and congenial repasts.

Looming up close on the spectator's east are a group of gently crowned peaks — high hills might be a better term — Mounts Kasuga, Mikasa, Wakakusa and Takamado which form a permanent backdrop for the city of Nara. Today, a modern 16-kilometer drive connects them, and a drive along it on a clear day affords one with a fine view of the entire Yamato Plain. Various recreation facilities — lodges, camp-sites and eating establishments — have been erected along this road in the last few years, and they attract a growing number of visitors each year. The most prominent features of the local terrain, these modest peaks were a favorite landscape for the nobles of the Tempyô Period, who seem to have had strong feelings of intimacy and nostalgia for them. They are fondly described according to their varying aspects during the changing seasons, and they seem to have influenced the moods of the courtiers at times, for the sentiments and emotions expressed in many of the *Manyôshû* poems seem to have been evoked by the appearance of the peaks under different weather conditions. The famous scholar Abe-no-Nakamaro, who traveled to China in 716 to study, and remained for the larger portion of his life, composed a poem on one occasion when he was homesick for his native land. In it, he longed for the sight of Mount Mikasa, a fact that suggests the symbolic importance of the peak for the Japanese of the eighth century.

Roughly a kilometer north of the towering Great Buddha Hall lie the upper reaches of a small river, the Saho River, which is mentioned in no less than 10 of the poems of the *Manyôshû*.

> At the Saho River crossing
> Where the plovers cry .....
> When shall I come for you,
> Fording the crystal-pure shallows
> On horseback .....

The supply of water seems to have been insufficient at Heijô Capital, and it has been suggested that this was one of the factors taken into consideration in the court's decision to move the capital to Heian (present Kyoto) at the end of the eighth century. Whether this is true or not, it is certain that the water around Nara does not compare with that at Kyoto, and the fact that the Saho River flows close to the site where the palace was located must have served to endear the modest stream to the court nobles. Thus, the fresh quiet beauty of the stream, with its abundance of plovers and frogs whose sounds made its banks so pleasant for the nobility of the eighth century, is repeatedly referred to in the poems. The lack of other rivers in the neighbourhood made the Saho River a point of particular focus in the urbane activities of the court members, who seem to have taken particular pleasure in boating excursions, and on occasion they allowed the leisurely current to carry them as far as distant Naniwa (present Osaka). An Edo Period (1615-1867) guide to the picturesque sights of Nara lists the "Fireflies of Saho River", and the river seems thus to have continued to have been renowned among the local residents over the centuries. The famous *O-mizutori* event, which is claimed to have taken place annually, without interruption, over the last 1,200 years at the Tôdai Temple, is one of the most interesting religious functions held in the Nara region. According to tradition, the priests who participate in the ceremony prepare for it by washing themselves in lustral water taken from the Ebisu River, one of the upper tributaries of the Saho River, another evidence that its waters have a reputation for being particularly pure.

Today the Saho River flows over the same bed and along the same course it pursued during the Tempyô Period, but there is little left of its pastoral beauty. Its supply of water noticeably diminished, it flows sluggishly down through the northern corner of the city, and on to the west. By the time it reaches a point south of the Heijô Palace site, there is no resemblance to the stream of the eighth century which was such a delight to the courtiers, for its water is mud-filled and stagnant. Rows of cherry trees stand along the embankments which have guided the stream's course over the centuries, and every spring they used to form a bright tunnel of blossoms; in recent years, however, many of them have withered with age and their appearance today is a generally forlorn one. These trees were originally planted by officials during the last part of the Edo Period in order to recall the traditions of the past and restore the beauty of the Saho region, and to pass this heritage on for the enjoyment of future generations. They naturally hoped that the trees would be replaced as they grew old, and the lovely atmosphere of the area maintained. Unfortunately, the officials of today seem to be interested only in encouraging the development of modern tourist facilities and factories, and such matters as the replacement of cherry trees appear to be too trifling for their consideration. This melancholy fact reveals one of the essential problems in Nara today — the gradual disappearance of Nara's traditional atmosphere of exquisite natural beauty and serenity. Many people have complained, but the juggernaut of commercialism continues to gain momentum, and each year is marked by the sad loss of some additional portion of the natural beauty cherished and preserved over the centuries.

To the north of the Saho region lies a low string of hills: Mounts Saho, Kurogami, Nara, and Saki. Atop Mount Kurogami is situated a unique post-war addition to the local landscape — "Dreamland" — Japan's own glorious interpretation of far-away Disneyland, with its impressive collection of treats for the common man and his children. Spread out over an area of roughly 25 acres fashioned by slashing the top off the hill, it contains a melange of recreational facilities designed to delight the most truculent youngster — a street from a Wild West town; a zooming roller coaster and a new screw coaster; a huge imitation of the Matterhorn, whose snow-capped crags remain unchanged even during the sweltering summer months; the adventurous Jungle Course, replete with terrifying plastic natives who challenge visitors with blood-curdling shouts, and paper-maché lions and elephants who roar and trumpet at regular intervals through the miracles of modern electronics. Surprisingly enough, a few argumentative souls have expressed a preference for the natural beauty of the hill before the introduction of this recreational paradise, and there has been some controversy over the "vulgarization" of Nara, although their pleas seem to be largely ineffective when they are balanced against the imposing weight of hard cash.

During the eighth century, the private residences of the nobles and officials of the court were located in the secluded area along the foot of this group of hills, and the region is fondly mentioned in a number of the *Manyôshû* poems. Some years ago, in fact, the actual remains of a number of residences, systematically laid out along what is presumed to have been an officials' street during Nara times, were unearthed in the grounds of a local high school located at the foot of Mount Nara, and an ancient well site in the area produced the remains of some wooden shoes of the sort which were worn by officials at the time. Also situated in the area is the Futai Temple, where Emperor Heijô retired after he was unsuccessful in regaining the throne and re-establishing it at Nara after it had been moved to Heian (present Kyoto) in 794. The courtier, poet and painter Ariwara-no-Narihira (823-880), whose romantic exploits are supposedly portrayed in the *Tales of Ise* (some of the chapters may well have been written by him), is traditionally said to have enjoyed the serenity of the Futai Temple and to have resided there, and the temple is also popularly known as the Ariwara Temple for this reason.

Running through the Saho area is Ichijô-dôri, an unimpressive road today, but a principal thoroughfare during the Tempyô Period. Traveling west along it, one passes two historic temples whose origins go back to the eighth century, the Kairyûô Temple and the Hokke Temple. The road continues until it reaches the site of the Heijô Palace, the center of the capital for over 70 years, during which seven rulers ascended the throne. Inside it were located the official residences of the monarchs and many of their court members as well as the most important offices of government and the headquarters for various authorities. This extensive area, which covers a square area enclosing eight blocks, measures 800 meters on each side. Today there is little to suggest the glories of the past or the superb architecture that graced the site except a commemorative marker and the slight elevations that mark the raised platforms where some of the buildings stood. The earth in the region is rich farmland, and the majority of the site now lies under cultivated fields except for about 25 acres which is covered with grass. While it is true that the neighborhood has a certain atmosphere of desolation about it on a grey day, one has no feeling that it has been forgotten or deserted by man, as is the case with many locations of historical importance, for the neat fields and carefully tilled crops give it an ordered, almost garden-like quality, and the palace grounds seem to slumber, oblivious, just below the fertile covering of soil. On a warm day in early summer, the peasants may be seen standing knee-deep in the flooded fields, laboriously transplanting the young rice shoots one by one in crisp straight lines across the broad area where many of the significant events of eighth century history occurred. At this time, and again in the autumn, when the tall, waving sea of dark green is being harvested, one is inclined to pause for a moment to reminisce about the continuity of man's activities, and the great antiquity of the Nara region, truly the "Cradle of Japanese Civilization".

THE TÔDAI TEMPLE AND
JAPANESE BUDDHISM

The introduction of Buddhism into Japan is traditionally assigned a date in the middle of the sixth century, when a Buddha image, together with volumes of sutras, banners and other regalia were dispatched from the kingdom of Paikche, located in the south-west region of the Korean Peninsula. The king of Paikche included a message of whole-hearted recommendation on behalf of the creed together with his gifts, urging the Japanese monarch to adopt it, praising its wisdom, merits, and efficacy, but pointing out that there were difficulties in comprehending the abstruse doctrine. Although Emperor Kinmei seems to have been duly impressed, Buddhism was not immediately propagated, for the proponents of the indigenous cult recognized it as a serious competitor to their native deities, and the possibilities for its success in Japan seemed very dim at first. A plague broke out, and the opponents of Buddhism were quick to suggest that the malign presence of the foreign image had offended the indigenous gods, and the Buddha figure was ignominiously thrown into Naniwa Canal and its crude temple burned. Nevertheless, certain individuals, notably members of the influential Soga Clan, were inclined toward the religion, in large part, it seems, for political reasons, and Buddhism had gained a foothold by the last quarter of the century. During the reign of Emperor Yômei (r. 585-587), who favored the creed, Buddhism gained momentum, and it advanced rapidly thereafter. Priests, temple carpenters, image makers, relics, documents, and statues began to arrive from Korea in growing numbers, and the faith gained power steadily. Its firm establishment, however, took place under the reign of Empress Suiko (r. 593-628) at the hands of Prince Umayado, commonly known today by his posthumous title, Prince Shôtoku. Inclined toward scholarship from his childhood, this pious nobleman devoted his efforts not only to the propagation of Buddhism, but also to studying the Chinese Classics, concepts of government, and administrative principles. Under his direction and encouragement many monasteries, most notably the Shitennô Temple and the Hôryû Temple, were erected, and philosophical and moral principles of the faith flowed directly into the mainstream of Japanese civilization, enriching it in innumerable ways.

Communication with the Korean Peninsula became more frequent, and emmissaries visited China. Buddhist clerics and artisans, still mainly from the Korean Kingdoms, but including an occasional Chinese, came to Japan in gradually increasing numbers and disseminated their knowledge and techniques to the eager Japanese. By 624, 46 temples and monastery compounds had been completed. The amazing progress of the faith during the course of the seventh century is apparent when one compares this figure with the one for the year 692, when 545 had been erected. The size of the compounds, their buildings, and the number and variety of the works of art they contained grew proportionately, and one can gain an idea of the scale of a major monastery of the late seventh century from the Yakushi Temple, whose dimensions appear to be essentially unchanged from those of the original site in the Asuka Area, where construction was begun in 680. With the establishment of the capital at Heijô (present Nara), however, the scale, complexity, and lavishness of the new monasteries continued to grow, until they occasionally challenged even the standards of the T'ang Dynasty continental prototypes. Most ambitious of these was the Tôdai Temple, which was clearly the wealthiest and most powerful religious center of the day. A network of provincial temples was established throughout the country during the eighth century at official court order. These temples came to play an important part in the direction of official affairs on the local level, and the Tôdai Temple's role as the headquarters for this system gave it considerable influence in the nation's administration and formulation of policy. Begun in 745, the completion of the huge Tôdai Temple compound required a decade and a half, and its construction and outfitting appears to have seriously strained the resources of the entire nation. Laid out on an unprecedented scale, its symmetrically oriented compound sprawled over an area more than ten miles square, and included architectural features and elaboration of plan never before attempted in Japan. Most conspicuous were the two soaring seven-storied pagodas, each bounded by its own enclosure, which reached 325 feet into the sky. Center of focus was the immense Daibutsu-den (Great Buddha Hall), which, in spite of its reduction in scale during subsequent reconstructions, remains the largest wooden building in the world.

The chief object of worship and veneration in this massive edifice was the huge image of Birushana Buddha, the principal deity of the Kegon sect. An epidemic of small-pox which struck in 737 and took a fearful toll throughout the country, including a sizeable group from the court and aristocracy, seems to have stimulated Emperor Shômu's initial decision to have the great figure cast. The erection of the image was intended as an appeal for relief to the Buddhist deities, who were implored to cure the sickness and restore conditions to normalcy. Lack of funds and the skilled technicians necessary for such an ambitious undertaking held up the project for some years. The first attempt at casting took place some distance from Nara at Shigaraki, in 745, but this ended in failure. The operation was subsequently shifted to Nara, where work on the image was begun in 747. Emperor Shômu himself is said to have filled his sleeves with dirt and symbolically assisted in the carrying of earth for the huge platform necessary for the project. The tremendous task of casting the figure, which took over two years, and was divided into eight stages, was finally completed under the supervision of a specialist of Korean descent in October of 749. The discovery of gold in Mutsu Province during the year was regarded as a particularly auspicious omen, and a large amount of the rare metal was sent to Nara for gilding the image. A special service of gratitude was held before the great figure, attended by the Emperor, his family and various high dignitaries. The Emperor assumed a position facing north, symbolizing his role as a subject of the Buddha, and an Imperial rescript was read in which the sovereign's words were phrased in humble language, and he spoke of himself as the servant of the Three Treasures of Buddhism. On April 9th of 752, the sumptuous Eye-opening Ritual dedication ceremony was held, marking the final completion of the immense gilded image. Attending the ceremony were Shômu, who had abdicated to become a Buddhist monk, his consort Kômyô, and the reigning Empress Kôken, together with members of the court and a vast throng of clerics which included a group of foreigners from countries as far distant as India and Central Asia. Some idea of the magnificence of the occasion may be gained from the contents of the Shôsôin Imperial Repository which contains many of the regalia objects and equipment used at the ceremony, including the brush used to symbolically open the immense eyes, which were almost four feet in length. This brush was wielded by Brahman Sôjô, an Indian priest, and to it were attached brightly colored strings which were held by prominent members of the assemblage so that they might participate symbolically in the ritual. When this was finished, a variety of gorgeous dances were performed, accompanied by throngs of musicians. The reading of sutras and other rites continued on into the night. Over 10,000 priests are said to have participated in the day's proceedings, and the ceremony continued on through the following day. The power and influence of the faith had reached a paramount position, and it was, in practice, if not officially, the religion of the court. The ceremony marked a high point in the fortunes of the religion in Japan.

History has dealt with the Great Buddha in a particularly

uncharitable manner. The first of a long series of calamities occurred in the ninth century when the colossal head, which had been cast in one piece, toppled to the ground during an earthquake. The image suffered severe damage during two disastrous fires which reduced the Great Buddha Hall to ashes, first in 1180, and again in 1567. Three years after the first halocaust, which was carried out by Taira soldiers in retaliation for the opposition of Tôdai Temple monks who had sided with the Minamoto forces, a Chinese artisan arrived in Nara to direct the recasting of the disfigured head. The head was ruined again following the second conflagration, and recast, but only after the remains of the great image had stood exposed to the elements for more than a century. Because of this melancholy history of repeated ruin and repair, little but the monumental dimensions of the present image remain to give the spectator an idea of the imposing original. Small portions of the legs and lower torso, and some of the petals of the lotus throne are all that remain of the original today, but the beautiful engraved scenes on the petals, which show a group of Buddhist deities rendered in rhythmic, elliptical, Baroque curves, reveal a close indebtedness to T'ang Chinese prototypes. The image sits cross-legged on a lotus throne which is 10 feet high and 68 feet across, and its ponderous bulk, which soars up over 53 feet, terminates just short of the massive cross-beams of the roof. Its titanic mass weighs nothing less than 500 tons!

On the periodic occasions when the Great Buddha is cleaned, the activities begin early in the morning. The 30 priests and assistants start by taking a bath at six o'clock, after which they don special white robes for the ritual. They then commence the prodigious task of dusting and washing the mountain of metal. The head and upper torso are reached by sitting in bamboo baskets which are suspended from the roof beams, while a ladder is used to climb up to the massive out-stretched left hand, the palm of which is the size of a small room in a Japanese house in area. During the course of the day, about 30 buckets full of dust are removed from the gigantic figure, and although it is impressive under normal circumstances, the juxtaposition of the minute white-clad figures against the dark mass of the image leaves the spectator with an unforgettable impression of its size. The job is finally completed around sundown; the priests and spectators retire, and the Great Buddha once again sits immaculate in the quiet evening gloom.

EXCAVATION OF THE HEIJÔ PALACE SITE

West of the present city of Nara lies the site of the eighth century palace — a huge area once filled with the residences of the nobility and the administrative offices of the government. Today, with the exception of a stone commemorative marker, nothing visible remains to suggest the splendour and size of the compound, for all of the fine buildings disappeared from the site well over a thousand years ago and most of the rich earth in the area was soon reclaimed by the peasants as farmland. In 1959, however, a five-year excavation plan was initiated under Government auspices to investigate a section of the site, and digging was finally begun under the careful supervision of an outstanding group of archaeologists. As the project progressed, relics began to come to light in ever increasing numbers, and the results so exceeded the expectations of the specialists that the plan was extended to ten years. The great wealth of finds which have been unearthed recently, however, have made it apparent that the task cannot be completed even in that time, and the decision has been made to continue investigations as long as is necessary. It is estimated that approximately 20% of the work has been accomplished to date and that 50 to 100 years will be necessary to bring this prodigious task to full completion.

The largest part of the excavation work was formerly carried out during two periods of the year – in the bitterest part of winter when chilling winds sweep down from the heights of Mount Ikoma and across the Nara Plain, and during the sweltering heat of summer which is typical of the Yamato Basin. The reason for this was that 80% of the area was cultivated farmland that could only be dug up during the fallow seasons, and because most of the workers on the site were farmers of the area. But now almost the entire site has been purchased by the government, making it possible to continue with the excavation work throughout the entire year.

The history of the palace itself extended over the reigns of seven monarchs – approximately 70 years. During this time a series of buildings were erected, removed, and new ones erected on the grounds according to alternate plans. Furthermore, during the reign of Emperor Shômu (r. 724-748), the location of the Imperial Palace was alternately shifted between Nara and several other areas some distance away. Among the stratified soil layers, scholars believe that there are the remains of at least ten successive architectural phases, and there are fascinating, if perplexing problems in determining their complex sequence and chronological order, as well as in reconstructing the original layout of the area from the evidence of the pillar bases, foundation stones, and drainage ditches. Archaeologists, depending almost entirely on the evidence of changes in the color and chemical make-up of the soil layers and the interrelationships of stratigraphy, have been able to divide the finds into groups based on 10 year divisions, stretching over the 70 odd years the splendid palace graced the area, and their diligent efforts and considerable skill have produced a series of impressively accurate results.

One day the investigators discovered a site which promised to be of particular interest. Mixed together in muddy confusion were a variety of fragments — potsherds in great numbers, and odds and ends of wood. A cursory glance at the objects was all that was necessary to confirm the scholar's first excited conclusion that they had stumbled on nothing less than an eighth century refuse pit, a veritable archaeological treasure trove which promised to supplement and clarify their knowledge of the implements and daily life of the palace during the Nara Period. As the sherds and other contents were slowly rescued from the muddy solution which had preserved them over the centuries, one of the scholars picked up a soaked wood fragment. About to cast it aside, he casually glanced at it. Somehow it struck him as being peculiar, and he noticed that it seemed to have been fashioned by human hands with some particular function in mind. After it was carefully washed, the fragment, only about 20 centimeters long, revealed itself to be a section of a wooden tally. Its condition was amazing for a wood object so long under the ground; indeed, the clearness of the grain was like that of a piece of wood buried in the earth less than a week. Most amazing, however, were the traces of writing on the fragment. The scholars began to study the characters, written in *sumi* ink, and by deciphering them one by one, they were finally able to make out a complete sentence. Highly elated by their discovery, the archaeologists turned their attention back to the pit, and, in

113

the ensuing days, they were able to recover almost 40 similar examples bearing Chinese characters. For over 1,200 years the wooden tallies had remained interred in the moist mud, as perfectly protected from the ageing effects of the atmosphere as if they had been placed in an air-tight can! However, when the mud was removed and the tallies were allowed to dry, the dark brown of the characters soon began to change in color. Somehow, it was reminiscent of the Japanese folk tale of *Urashima Tarô*, a young boy from a fishing village who one day rescued a huge sea turtle from some mischievous children, and was rewarded for his kindness by being escorted to the enchanted Dragon Palace deep below the ocean. There, he passed many happy days in the company of the queen of the palace whose charms were such that he entirely forgot about his village and his parents. One day he remembered, however, and set out to return, carrying a gift from the queen — a small box which he was instructed not to open. When he reached home, however, all was changed — sights as well as people — and, disillusioned, he sat down on the beach and opened the box. Immediately, a white vapor arose from the box, his beard turned white, and he became an aged man dressed in threadbare clothing. Similarly, the characters on the wooden tallies, exposed to the atmosphere after centuries of dark sanctuary, returned somehow to the temporal world of passing time, with its rules of birth, longevity and demise, began to fade. To arrest this process the tallies were immediately put in plastic bags and placed in a refrigerator filled with a formalin preservative. Then research on their inscriptions was continued.

They range in size from 50x3 centimeters to diminutive examples measuring only about 10 centimeters in length and 1 in width. The contents of the writing fall into two general categories: communications and messages within the palace, together with requests and chits for various commodities issued by its officials; and receipts for the arrival of baggage containing tax payments-in-kind from the various provinces. Thus, one medium sized specimen contained a matter of fact inscription written by a woman official named Lady Chikuba, apparently authorizing the bureau in charge of palace stores to deliver some provisions, red beans, soy sauce, vinegar, and miso-paste to a certain Buddhist temple. This record is of particular interest for there is an entry in the *Shoku Nihongi*, an early historical chronicle, which mentions a woman official known as Chikuba who served as the superintendent of the Imperial Kitchen during the reign of Empress Kôken (749-758), and there can be little doubt that they are the same person. The foodstuffs mentioned on the tally suggest that someone from the palace, possibly Empress Kôken herself, spent some time in residence at a temple during this period.

Princess Abe, the daughter of Emperor Shômu and Empress Kômyô, ascended the throne as the ruling empress in 749 with the name Empress Kôken, succeeding her father, who took the tonsure. During the fourth year of her reign, the greatest event of the century, the ceremony celebrating the final completion of the Great Buddha of the Tôdai Temple was held, and she officiated at the elaborate festivities together with her parents. At about this time, her relationship with her minister Fujiwara-no-Nakamaro became intimate, and he came to exercise an ever increasing influence over her decisions. When the great ceremony was ended, she did not return directly to the palace; rather, she went to Nakamaro's residence, where she remained for some time. She was 35 and in the prime of life, and from this time on she made frequent trips to the minister's residence. Although her behavior elicited considerable attention, the relationship grew increasingly close after the death of her father, Emperor Shômu, and, overcome with devotion for her lover, she had the legitimate heir to the throne set aside, and designated Nakamaro's favorite, Ôi, as crown prince in his stead. Under the protective favor of her patronage, Nakamaro's power and influence grew steadily, and their intimacy continued over a span of 10 years. In the autumn of 761, however, the Empress, who had abdicated in 758 in favor of Prince Ôi, fell ill. During the 8 month period of her convalescence, she unexpectedly fell under the charms of a monk named Dôkyô, who is said to have assisted her considerably in her recuperation. Her affections shifted entirely, and after her recovery, the 44 year old monarch was so much swayed by the influence of the ambitious bonze that she turned a deaf ear to the protestations of her former lover Nakamaro. She returned to the capital in the following year accompanied by Dôkyô; her break with Nakamaro became final, and her opposition to Emperor Junnin (Prince Ôi) grew. According to the *Shoku Nihongi*, she set up her residence at the Hokke Temple, summoned all officials above the Fifth Rank, and publicly declared that Emperor Junnin would henceforth deal only with ceremonial affairs while she herself would attend to all government matters of importance. The conflict between the two factions finally erupted into combat, and Nakamaro's forces, after being defeated in a sortie at the capital, led to Ômi where they were overtaken on the shore of Lake Biwa, and their leader ignominiously slain by two of his cousins. The unfortunate emperor, deserted by his troops and followers, was deprived of his title and banished to Awaji Island, where he was strangled a short time afterwards. The Empress then reassumed the throne under the name Empress Shôtoku, a remarkable event which began a turbulent era in which the intractable Dôkyô's influence over her became so great that he came very close to realizing his objective and acquiring the throne for himself.

But, to return to the wooden tally and the matter of its request for foodstuffs from the Imperial stores. To begin with, the temple mentioned must be the Hokke Temple. The date written on the tally is the 6th of March, and the year must be either 762 when the Empress returned to the capital accompanied by Dôkyô, the following year, 763, or 764, when she again took the throne. Thus, this modest fragment of wood, buried in the mud of a refuse pit, lies before us, a remarkably preserved reminder of the dramatic events of the Nara Period 1,200 years ago.

At a location in the north of the Imperial Palace site, scholars have uncovered an area where a palace kitchen enclosure appears to have originally stood; adjoining it are the remains of a well which has been of particular interest. No obvious signs of its presence were visible at first, for it was completely filled with earth, but its location was eventually betrayed by a slight variation in the color of the soil. The members of the excavation team set to work, and as they carefully removed the miscellanea of the centuries from its interior, it became increasingly clear that it was not a common well. A beautifully fitted framework, square in shape and made of thick planks of Japanese cypress, lined the shaft. And as the digging continued, remnants of various types of pottery fragments began to come to light. Although many of the sherds were broken into very small pieces, they were taken back to the excavation headquarters and laid out for study. The team members soon found that it was possible, after very careful matching, to reconstruct a number of the vessels, and this exacting task was continued, usually when there was some break in the actual excavation work, over a considerable period of time. Finally, indications that the digging was approaching the bottom of the well began to appear, and the members began to discover other objects among the sherds.

The coins recovered from the well presented an interesting sampling of the currency in use during the eighth century. Most numerous were counterfeit imitations of the *Wadô-kaichin* series of 708, which appear to have had a considerable circulation during the period. The economic history of the Nara Period is characterized by a relentless inflationary cycle; the prices of commodities soared and the buying power of money decreased to a small fraction of its original value. In order to correct this unfortunate imbalance, other series were cast and put into circulation, such as the *Mannen-tsûhô* coins, which date from 760, three of which came to light in the well. In an attempt to increase the buying power of currency, the government established an arbitrarily high value to this new coinage, one to ten of the old *Wadô-kaichin* series. It does not seem to have been long afterward that this ratio grew considerably less, however. Three specimens of a slightly later series (*Jingû-kaihô*), issued in 765, were also found, and demonstrate that the government was still continuing its attempts to counter inflation by issuing new coinage. By 772, however, the three coinages seem to have been used interchangeably, and although a further series, known as *Ryûhei-eihô*, was issued in 796 after the capital had been shifted away from Nara to the new metropolis at the Heian Capital (present Kyoto), the old *Wadô-kaichin* coins seem to have been the most highly valued among the common populace, whose confidence in the value of the series is demonstrated by the fact that it was widely saved. Although the new capital at Kyoto was established in 794 by Emperor Kanmu, his two successors, Emperors Heijô and Saga, favored a return of the capital to Nara, and both of them resided in the old capital at one time or another. Their efforts were unsuccessful in the end, but the recovery of a single *Ryûhei-eihô* coin seems to indicate that the well was still in use, and possibly supplying water to an Imperial Kitchen close-by about the turn of the century.

The most unusual relic recovered from the well was a small wooden doll, measuring 15 centimeters in length by about 2.5 centimeters in width. It is very simply fashioned, and the legs are crudely set into the torso. As a work of art, its value is negligible at best; in the study of the customs of the eighth century however, its interest is considerable, for it seems to have been used with a particular purpose in mind — to bring misfortune to some adversary or foe. Small wooden nails were driven into both eyes and the bosom of the doll, and something had been written on its torso. Although the characters are too faded to be legible, there can be little doubt that the inscription constituted a malediction of some sort. A moustache was painted on the face so the figure must have represented a man, although there is no clue as to his identity. Nor is there any indication whether it was a man or a woman who wished him evil. There were certainly numerous occasions during the Nara Period when one person might have wished to place a curse on the life of another, for the entire era is marked by machinations, intrigues, and the ill feelings of individuals conspiring against one another for power and influence. In the end however, what is most striking to the student of Nara history is that, in spite of the repeated occurrence of such melancholy episodes, the various institutions of government made noteable progress during the eighth century and the culture which bloomed with such strength and beauty during the period left a fragrance which is still impressively apparent 1,200 years later.

THE NARA DEER

Visitors to Nara are invariably pleased by the sight of the deer who graze peacefully in the broad, grass-covered areas around the Kôfuku Temple, the Tôdai Temple, and Kasuga Shrine. Deer have been present in the Japanese Archipelago since long before mankind made his appearance, and some of the earliest evidences of man's habitation in the Islands are accompanied by artifacts formed from the horns and bones of deer. Archaeologists have recovered such implements in great numbers from pre-pottery sites, as well as Jômon pottery locations, and it is clear that man was particularly dependent on the animal for many of his daily needs. Again, deer are mentioned frequently in the poems of the classic anthology, the *Manyôshû,* where they are admired for their gentleness.

According to the records of Kasuga Shrine, its foundation dates to 767, when it was set up by Fujiwara-no-Nagate as the tutelary shrine of the powerful Fujiwara clan. Four gods are enshrined, and the foremost of these, Takemikatsuchi-no-kami, was brought from Kashima in Hitachi Province riding on the back of a white deer. For this reason, the animal acquired a special status in Kasuga Shrine, where it serves as a divine messenger to the shrine gods, and symbol of the institution as a whole. During the Heian Period (794-1185) when certain accommodations were made between Buddhism and the native Shintô faith, and many Shintô deities came to be regarded as manifestations of Buddhist gods, the famous Kasuga mandala was fashioned, and the white deer was used as its central representation. The idea of the celestial characteristic of the deer and their role as messengers of the gods became firmly established in Japanese thought during the period of Fujiwara prosperity and influence during the Heian Period, and even after the clan's decline, the idea continued, and the deer were protected by the local officials. This movement was also backed by the Kôfuku Temple, the tutelary temple of the Fujiwara Clan, and the protection of the animals became a fixed policy as well as a local custom.

Some idea of how strictly the regulations for the protection of these animals were enforced at times may be surmised from *Ishiko-tsume*, a traditional tale which is still narrated in some of the popular genre theatres in Japan. According to the story, Misaku, a youth of 13, was practicing calligraphy one day when a brash deer from Kasuga Shrine happened on the scene and nonchalantly proceeded to eat the boy's valuable copy book. Enraged at such rude behavior, he picked up his paper weight and hurled it at the animal, striking it square on the nose with such force that it killed the unfortunate beast. Misaku was condemned for his offense and the sentence was soon carried out; he was bound in the deer's carcass, and placed in a deep hole. Then stones were thrown in on top of him, burying the poor fellow alive, until he finally succumbed under the weight. To the present day, a site known as *Ishiko-tsume* remains, located just to the east of Sarusawa Pond. Although there is no proof to substantiate this tradition, the Kôfuku Temple records do mention a similar case. The entry appears in a document of the middle Edo Period and states that in 1664, a man was captured by the priests of the temple after he had killed one of the Kasuga deer, and after a hearing, he was taken to the Great South Gate (Nandai-mon) of the Kôfuku Temple where farewell rites were administered to him. He was then dressed in special attire and led about the walls of the temple compound. Following this, he was taken to the execution grounds at the Hannya Temple where he was beheaded. Although this is but a single instance, it does suggest the respect that was accorded the deer in Nara over the centuries.

Some time after the last cherry blossoms have fallen and the trees are filled with the bright green of new leaves, the first fawns are born. The foaling period continues into July. During this time, the does may be seen tending their newborn, strolling under the trees or resting quietly in the shade of one of the temple buildings. The fawns, who make their appearance in festive brown with a dappling of bright white, are able to stand within an hour of their birth. During this season, the ordinarily timid does become aggressive in the protection of their young, and will attack visitors who approach too closely.

When the greens have already begun to change to the rich browns, yellows and vibrant reds which make fall such a lovely time to be in Nara, one can hear the first plaintive, yet intense, calls of the stags that indicate that the mating season has finally arrived. Their horns are already hard and sharpened from diligent polishing against trees and in the earth, and from this day on, they may be seen daily, locking horns and battling to best their opponents. They push and butt with all the strength they can summon, but as the days pass, the combat inevitably exacts its toll until only the most powerful stags are left. The victors gather their harems about close by, jealously guarding them from the defeated stags who are finished fighting, but are still alert to the possibility of stealing a doe who strays too far from her group. During this period, when wild instincts are strongest in the stags, they think little of challenging humans as well as their fellows. It is in order to prevent such misfortunes that the horns are removed from the stags in an annual ceremony.

During the middle ages in Japan, when the religious power and influence of Kasuga Shrine and the Kôfuku Temple were at their peak, the status of the deer was such that they were treated with particular deference, and it is clear that their welfare was a matter of more importance than that of the common man. By the middle of the Edo Period, however, the social status of the ordinary individual had improved somewhat, and it seems that consideration was first given to the idea of annually removing the antlers from the stags in order to prevent the possibility of accidents and injuries to man. At the same time, it appears that cutting off the horns was also regarded as a means of protecting the deer themselves, and a document dating to 1671 contains an entry which seems to be the first record of such an event. The Nara townsmen can hardly be blamed for taking a particular delight in the initiation of this practice, for the resentment that had accumulated over the centuries, during which they had been forced to endure the frequent mischief and occasional injury inflicted by the deer was undoubtedly deep-seated. For this reason, the annual ceremony took on an aura of a show for the local people, and we can easily imagine how they enjoyed seeing the haughty stags divested of their formidable weapons by the local officials and Kôfuku Temple priests.

Stands are erected about the middle of October in a cleared area adjacent to the pathway leading to Kasuga Shrine, and the ceremony takes place there. Decorative curtains adorned with heraldic emblems are hung about the arena, and the event is performed in an atmosphere which is festive, but somehow also imbued with a sense of religious ritual. On the day of the ceremony, the stags, who have been rounded up over the previous month, are driven into the enclosure in groups. Then the attendants, known as *seko*, who are dressed in dark blue coats bearing the wisteria crest of Kasuga Shrine, single them out, lasso them, and bind the reluctant deer – no small task considering the impressive size of the largest stags. After they are pacified — a job which frequently requires the combined efforts of all of the *seko* — their horns are carefully sawed off, and they are released. The disappearance of their symbol of pride and masculinity is clearly embarrassing to them, and they waste little time in fleeing to the sanctuary of the groves of trees nearby.

HOIKUSHA COLOR BOOKS

ENGLISH EDITIONS

Book Size 4″×6″

COLORED ILLUSTRATIONS FOR NATURALISTS

Text in Japanese, with index in Latin or English.

First Issues (Book Size 6″ × 8″)

1. BUTTERFLIES of JAPAN
2. INSECTS of JAPAN vol.1
3. INSECTS of JAPAN vol.2
4. SHELLS of JAPAN vol.1
5. FISHES of JAPAN vol.1
6. BIRDS of JAPAN
7. MAMMALS of JAPAN
8. SEA SHORE ANIMALS of JAPAN
9. GARDEN FLOWERS vol.1
10. GARDEN FLOWERS vol.2
11. ROSES and ORCHIDS
12. ALPINE FLORA of JAPAN vol.1
13. ROCKS
14. ECONOMIC MINERALS
15. HERBACEOUS PLANTS of JAPAN vol.1
16. HERBACEOUS PLANTS of JAPAN vol.2
17. HERBACEOUS PLANTS of JAPAN vol.3
18. SEAWEEDS of JAPAN
19. TREES and SHRUBS of JAPAN
20. EXOTIC AQUARIUM FISHES vol.1
21. MOTHS of JAPAN vol.1
22. MOTHS of JAPAN vol.2
23. FUNGI of JAPAN vol.1
24. PTERIDOPHYTA of JAPAN
25. SHELLS of JAPAN vol.2
26. FISHES of JAPAN vol.2
27. EXOTIC AQUARIUM FISHES vol.2
28. ALPINE FLORA of JAPAN vol.2
29. FRUITS
30. REPTILES and AMPHIBI-ANS of JAPAN
31. ECONOMIC MINERALS vol.2
32. FRESHWATER FISHES of JAPAN
33. GARDEN PLANTS of the WORLD vol.1
34. GARDEN PLANTS of the WORLD vol.2
35. GARDEN PLANTS of the WORLD vol.3
36. GARDEN PLANTS of the WORLD vol.4
37. GARDEN PLANTS of the WORLD vol.5
38. THE FRESHWATER PLANKTON of JAPAN
39. MEDICINAL PLANTS of JAPAN

⟨ENGLISH EDITIONS⟩

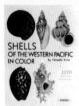

SHELLS
OF
THE
WESTERN
PACIFIC
IN
COLOR

Book Size 7″×10″

⟨vol. Ⅰ⟩ by Tetsuaki Kira
(304 pages, 72 in color)
⟨vol. Ⅱ⟩ by Tadashige Habe
(304 pages, 66 in color)

FISHES
OF
JAPAN
IN
COLOR

Book Size 7″×10″

by Toshiji Kamohara
(210 pages, 64 in color)